# WHAT DID YOUR
# PARENTS
## DO TO YOU?

# WHAT DID YOUR PARENTS DO TO YOU?

What Would You Say If You Were Asked How You Felt about the Childhood Experiences You Had with Your Parents?

Dr. Mattie Lee Jones

Copyright © 2019 by Dr. Mattie Lee Jones.

ISBN        Softcover        978-1-949723-55-7

All rights reserved. No part of this book may be reproduced or transmitted in any form or by any means, electronic or mechanical, including photocopying, recording, or by any information storage and retrieval system without express written permission from the author, except in the case of brief quotations embodied in critical reviews and certain other non-commercial uses permitted by copyright law.

Printed in the United States of America.

To order additional copies of this book, contact:
Bookwhip
1-855-339-3589
https://www.bookwhip.com

To my granddaughter, Raven Lee.
As you go through life, remember that I love you and that "with God all things are possible" (Mark 10:27 KJV).

# Contents

Acknowledgments . . . . . . . . . . . . . . . . . . . . . . . . . . . . ix

Introduction . . . . . . . . . . . . . . . . . . . . . . . . . . . . . . . . . xi

Survivors . . . . . . . . . . . . . . . . . . . . . . . . . . . . . . . . . . . . 1

Can the Cycle of Damage Be Broken? . . . . . . . . . . . . . 21

Love Is the Key . . . . . . . . . . . . . . . . . . . . . . . . . . . . . . . 37

Intervening for a Broken Child . . . . . . . . . . . . . . . . . . 53

A Healing Exercise . . . . . . . . . . . . . . . . . . . . . . . . . . . . 61

Final Reflections . . . . . . . . . . . . . . . . . . . . . . . . . . . . . 67

Bibliography . . . . . . . . . . . . . . . . . . . . . . . . . . . . . . . . 71

About the Author . . . . . . . . . . . . . . . . . . . . . . . . . . . . 73

# Acknowledgments

To all birth parents, foster parents, grandparents, and guardians: please know that you play a powerful and irreplaceable role in developing physically, socially, and emotionally healthy children.

God bless all those who shared their stories.

# Introduction

What did your parents do to you? Whether positive or negative, your parents had a hand in molding you. Outside influences that were out of your parents' control, such as bullying, peer pressure, and contact with other adults (teachers, relatives), also helped shape who you are and how you react to life. Not to devalue those outside forces, this book's main focus is on the role parents play. I define parents as anyone who is legally responsible for the care of a child and those with whom the child lives.

After over twenty years of talking to parents about children as an educator, school principal, and parenting trainer, I have heard it all. I find it interesting that parents reflect back to their own childhoods when dealing with their children. Parents have told me how they hated certain things their parents did to them, but they ended up doing the same things to their children.

The stories I heard in recent years as a parenting trainer inspired me to document and share some of their experiences. In the following chapters I share real-life childhood stories of people who answered the question "What did your parents do to you?" These stories contain discussions, quotes, and opinions concerning how childhood experiences affected them as children and throughout their adult lives.

For confidentiality, the names of those telling their stories have been changed. I do not reveal the names of family members. The people telling their stories were informed that they would not be compensated monetarily or in any other way. I did not use any scientific methods to select the people, and not all of the stories are included. Over the period of about two years, I interviewed and had conversations with people I met on my own, was introduced to, or already knew. During interviews and conversations I took notes and used a tape recorder. I was granted permission to share the stories in this book. To prevent redundancy, I

## INTRODUCTION

selected stories that I felt covered the highest possibility of experiences that people could identify with.

It is my purpose to stimulate conversations about what parents have done and are doing to their children and to make parents realize that whether their impact on their children is positive, negative, intentional, or unintentional, they are responsible for the results of their parenting—or lack of parenting—on their children. This is done by following the journeys of those who allowed me to look through the windows of their childhood. Some are stories of survival, while others are stories of celebration, appreciation, and intervention.

The stories inspired the titles for the various chapters, and those titles categorize the types of events experienced.

The stories also reveal how the people telling them felt their experiences with their parents affected them emotionally and socially, as well as the positive effects of unconditional love and the negative effects of abuse. The following define unconditional love and describe abuse as they pertain to the stories in this book:

Dictionary.com defines unconditional love as "affection with no limits or conditions; complete love."

An article in the *Columbia Electronic Encyclopedia* titled "Child Abuse—Causes and Effects 2012" described child abuse as

> Physical, sexual, or emotional maltreatment or neglect of children by parents, guardians, or others responsible for a child's welfare. Physical abuse is characterized by physical injury, usually inflicted as a result of a beating or inappropriately harsh discipline. Sexual abuse includes molestation, incest, rape, prostitution, or use of a child for pornographic purposes. Neglect can be physical in nature (abandonment, failure to seek needed health care), educational (failure to see that a child is attending school), or emotional (abuse of a spouse or another child in the child's presence, allowing a child to witness adult substance abuse). Inappropriate punishment, verbal abuse, and scapegoating are also forms of emotional or psychological child abuse. Some authorities consider parental actions abusive if they have negative future consequences.

## INTRODUCTION

The journey of becoming an adult carries many natural struggles and confusing times. Making it through childhood can be aided or complicated by parents. It is my desire that *What Did Your Parents Do to You?* will encourage parents to think about how they are rearing their children, prevent the experiences that can be damaging, and be used as a tool for personal healing and enlightenment.

Some people survive being damaged as a child and some don't. In the chapter "Survivors" you will read different stories of adults who consider themselves survivors. They talk about the negative experiences they had with their parents and the process of healing that they feel took them a lifetime to accomplish.

Most people believe there was nothing wrong with the way their parents interacted with them because that type of interaction was all they knew. In the chapter "Can the Cycle of Damage Be Broken?" you will read the stories of people who as adults are still healing from the physical and emotional abuse they experienced as children. They share how they became determined to find a way to break the cycle of abuse that exists in their families. A story of unconditional love is shared in "Love

Is the Key." Other stories reflect how both negative and positive family experiences influence lives. You will also hear a story of how children who grew up in the same home had different experiences of both love and hate with the same parents.

It has been said that if you can heal a child, you don't have to spend years repairing an adult. In the chapter "Intervening for a Broken Child" I tell a story that I created to demonstrate the importance of intervening for children who are being damaged. This is the only story that is fictional. It is a combination of different stories I had been told that I felt had similar meanings and outcomes.

Children have been compared to arrows and their parents to bows. What parents do to and for their children sends them in that same direction. Some children are broken arrows before they even get out of the quiver; that is, they are broken before they leave home. My more than five years of formal and informal research on the perspectives of parents has revealed to me that most all parents interact with their children the same way their parents interacted with them. Many of the parents I spoke with shared that they did not know what to do with their children or if they were doing the right things. This inspired me to start the nonprofit company Parent Link Inc. (www.parentlinkinc.org). Parent Link's goal is to prevent the physical, social, and emotional damage of children by supporting and training parents.

As adults we sometimes duplicate the experiences we had as children, even the negative ones. We become the very thing we hated in our parents, and this can mean inflicting the same hurt on our children that we experienced. I believe this happens because our brains have accepted the things that we live through as normal or comfortable because these things are familiar to us. To change, even though it may make life better, is hard. Our minds may find the transformation uncomfortable and seek to return to what we have known and consider normal. I believe parents' damaging behavior can be passed down from generation to generation because of this mind-set.

An example of this mind-set comes from a parent in one of my Parent Link training sessions who explained that she had tried one of the communication strategies with her child that she'd learned in the session. She normally yelled when her child misbehaved, and she found it hard to stop. She said she was uncomfortable trying the new strategies because yelling was the way her mother responded to her, and she did not feel her child would get the point if she did not yell at her.

Parenting is not easy. Parents do the best they can with what they know. They strive to give their children positive experiences. However, parents intentionally and unintentionally have negative experiences with their children. Children can survive the damage, such as poor nurturing and abusive situations, but just because they continue to live, it does not mean they will grow up to be whole, healthy adults. I pray that this book will serve as an inspiration for others to share their childhood stories.

- Telling your story leads to the path of healing.
- Telling your story gives cause to celebrate.
- Telling your story can inspire others.

# SURVIVORS

It is said that dysfunction has become acceptable in our society, so much so that it has been given names and labels and is displayed on television as entertainment in sitcoms, cartoons, and reality-television-profiled families in dysfunctional situations. *Webster's Dictionary* (11th ed.) defines dysfunctional as, "impaired or abnormal functioning." *Impair* means "to make worse; to diminish in quality, value, excellence, and strength; and to deteriorate." This definition leaves me pondering what type of deteriorating effects dysfunction has on children.

T. D. Jakes, a well-known pastor and author, discusses in one of his sermons how painful it is to have to try to get as a grown man what you should have gotten as a child. You may be trying to get it as an adult because your father didn't do what he should have done. Sometimes children have both a negative and positive relationship with their parents. The kind of negative, hurtful experiences that leave them feeling unloved mix with positive experiences that make them feel that their parents do care for and love them. These inconsistent interactions can cause a lot of confusion in their childhoods and even in their adult lives.

As we go through the journey of life, we search for answers to questions that no one seems to want to answer. When I asked Anthony what his parents did to him, he had both a negative and positive response. He said that when his father finally became a man, he helped Anthony become one and that his mother abandoned him.

## Anthony, age fifty, raised by a single divorced father

Anthony started his story by saying that the abandonment by his mother had the most negative impact on his life, because he did not know what was going on in his parents' relationship. When she left, he did not understand why she was the one to leave.

I was fourteen when she first left home, and we did not see her for several weeks. The second time she left for a short time, and my father got her to come back. The third time I was fifteen years old and she left for good. There were three of us in the house, two boys and one girl. When she left, I felt that the blame was on me. I also felt guilty, like maybe I had contributed something to my mom and dad falling out. I felt most hurt by my mom because I expected my father to be the one to do something, like leave us.

My dad was very high-strung and negative. My mom was not a negative person. She was very quiet. I thought my mother was the perfect mom. She was always doing things with us kids and teaching us things. So when she left, it was crushing. If you ask me what did my mom do to me, she crushed me; she took away my trust and security.

The one word I can use to describe the negative experience with my dad would be *irresponsible* because he drank heavily; and when he and my mother were together, he avoided his responsibility as a father. I thought he would be the one to leave us. I don't think I would have had the same reaction if it had been my dad. I still would have been upset because I was really about family. Even as a teenager I wanted my family together.

Anthony said that he was very depressed all through high school. He was sad, and a lot of his friends and people who knew him would comment on it. They would try to get him to talk.

I was very quiet. My only refuge was that I was going to school. In school I studied hard and worked hard in my books; and I got involved in sports, which helped as well.

Even though my father was still there, even though he stayed and took care of us, I did not feel secure. I never knew if one day he would not come home. But he stayed and was there for me during the critical time of my teen years. This was a time when as a boy I needed guidance in becoming a man. This was a positive experience with my father. He drew a line with us. I was very headstrong, but I would never cross the line with my father. When I would do something or consider doing something I was not supposed to do, I would always look at that line. That line was represented by a look my dad would give. He could look at me and I would think, *What would he think or do if I cross that line?*

Anthony said that eventually his mother took his sister (who was the youngest) to live with her. He felt okay about that but was still hurt and wondering what had happened. He wanted to know why he and his sister had to be in the middle and why whatever was going on with his parents had to happen.

I developed a general dislike for women. I was very bitter when I related to my mother. It got to the point that I did not want anything to do with my mother. I was the oldest, so before she took my sister, I was responsible for both my sister and brother. I cleaned the house, grocery shopped, and cooked. I became the wife in the house. I sat up with my dad and heard his stories through his drinking and through his tears.

There was times when we would visit my mother, and during the visits I would not talk to her. I did not want to visit her, but I would take my brother and sister to see her. It got to the point that some of my relatives got concerned and told me that I really needed to talk to my mother, because they could see the anger in me.

Anthony stated that the relationship he had with his mother spilled over into the relationships he had with other women. It came out in the way he treated them. An example he gave was that if a woman wanted to talk, he would not talk because of his negative view of women. He did not trust them. Another way he expressed this was in his response to friends when they had problems with women. He would always blame the women and not the guys. He said this was because of what he had gone through with his mother. His negative view of women also manifested itself when he met his wife.

He got married when he was twenty, and another phase of his healing from the past started.

I met my wife in college. She could see the anger in me toward women, and we had a discussion about it. With her I was able to talk about my childhood. We would share the experiences that we both had growing up, because she had gone through some things with her parents as well. She said that she could see that my relationship with other women was affected by what happened with my mother and that she understood but did not want to be disrespected in any way, so I really had to change.

When I married her and as we started to have children, I considered myself a survivor. It was not easy, but I became determined to break the cycle of hurt and pain by not allowing my past to determine my present relationship with my wife and children.

Years later, Anthony had to take a long car trip with his mother. They traveled from Chicago, Illinois, to Memphis, Tennessee. They went to Memphis to see his mother's mother, who was ill. He said that during the trip he and his mother talked like they had never talked before.

As we traveled, my mom began to disclose her relationship with her mother and my father. She told me that the pain she was going through with my father at the time did not allow her to reveal what she needed to reveal to me and that she was sorry she was not strong enough for us. Mom said that the things she regretted the most were not taking us to church and not putting her foot down with my dad. She shared that she was not in a place of strength in her life then and responded the only way she knew, and that was to get out . . . to run away.

My mom felt that being raised by an alcoholic mother contributed to her inability to cope with us. She told me that when she was a child, her mother was an alcoholic, and that she had abandoned her. I listened as Mom told me some of the things that happened to her as a child. When she was three years old, her mother left her, and she was found sitting on a bench with uncombed hair, dirty clothes, and eating a piece of old bread. She said that after that a lady she did not know adopted her. She was adopted by a lady that we grew up calling our grandmother.

Our conversation continued, with my mother telling me about the negative things that she went through with my father. Up to that time the only thing I had heard was put-downs about her from my father. I was only getting one side of the story. As she talked to me, I felt my eyes were opened for the first time, and I had to apologize for my anger toward her. Those conversations with her during that long trip down south helped me start to heal. I had walked around with a dark cloud over my head for many years.

What did my parents do to me? They made me want to be a parent that my children can trust, love, and respect. Even though I survived, I want to make their journey a better one. I want them to know who I am and that I love them.

Anthony's story of abandonment by his mother is not uncommon. Maya Angelou, in her book *Mom & Me & Mom*, shared a similar experience about the abandonment she felt when her mother sent her and her brother to live with their grandmother. When she later went back to be with her mother, her mother told her why she had left her.

Maya wrote that her mother told her she missed her but that she knew she would have been a terrible mother and they all would have been sorry if she had kept them.

One of the many passages in her book that I found inspiring is the following:

> Love heals. Heals and liberates. I use the word *love*, not meaning sentimentality, but a condition so strong that it may be that which holds the stars in their heavenly positions and that which causes the blood to flow orderly in our veins.

## Mark, age fifty-one, raised by both biological parents

Mark's story is a reflection of what can happen to a child exposed to dysfunctional behavior during childhood. Mark said that he survived what he felt was a dysfunctional and abusive childhood. His story is about his experience with his father and how that experience took him on a forty-year journey of forgiveness and healing. He is now a police officer and respected in his community.

I have found that what we cannot change or control, we try to label. Whether we label it dysfunctional or something else, there are a lot of things that happen in families that I feel parents should be held accountable for.

Mark shared that when he looks back over his life, he feels that over 90 percent of his experiences with his father were bad. Over the forty years of his life, he did not like his father for a period of time. He even got to the point when he could say that if there was one person in the world he hated, it was his father.

His story goes back to when he was eight years old. One hot summer day, at about eight in the morning, his father asked him if he wanted to go for a walk to Curly's store. Curly's was a small neighborhood store where his father would go to drink and gamble. Mark and his father went to the back of the store, which was on an alley, and his father went in.

After hours of standing outside the door waiting for his father to come out, Mark knocked on the door.

A man finally opened and asked, "Who is it?" I told the man what my name was. The man said, "Who are you?" I told him that my father was in there. The man then said that "there is no one here" and closed the door. I kept beating on the door, and the man came back and threatened to beat me if I did not stop beating on the door. I said again, "I am his son," while standing in the door. The man turned around to look back inside. As the man turned, I could see my father at a table three to five feet away, and I could tell that he had heard me. I said to myself, *I know he heard me!*

The man asked my father if he had someone waiting on him, and he said no. The man closed the door again, and I started to beat on it again and yelling for my father, saying, "I want to go home." The last time the man opened the door, I pointed and said, "That's my daddy right there." What my father said next really destroyed and damaged me.

I heard him say to the man, "I don't have a son." When he said he did not have a son, that broke my heart, and I cried all the way home and never told my mother or anyone.

Mark said that he internalized the anger he felt from that incident. No matter what his father had done before that day, Mark had still always wanted to bond with him. At that moment, the desire to bond was gone.

As a teenager I watched the things my father did, such as fussing and fighting with my mother, and the angrier I got. As I got older, I tried to lie to myself and say that it didn't matter but realized that it did. Because my father was drunk all the time, I could not stand the sight of him. I tried to give my father an excuse by saying that he did what he did because he was drunk, but I still felt that no matter what state my father was in, I wanted an apology or a hug or something. After graduating from high school, I went into the military. While there I did a lot of confidential things for the military that I only shared with my mother.

Mark continued his story by saying that when he came home once on military leave, his mother was sick in the hospital. His father came to the hospital drunk and was going to try to drive himself home. Mark made the decision to take his father home. While Mark was driving toward the highway exit, his father said out of nowhere, "Do you want to have a drink?" Thinking that his father might be trying to be okay, he said yes.

His father then cussed at him and said, "You will never drink with me. You are nothing. You are not on that level with me." He told his father that he was driving and really didn't want a drink. Still surprised at what had happened, he kept driving.

As I kept driving, I felt something on the side of my head at the temple area. At that moment I told myself not to move. *Don't move; don't think about what is happening. I cannot believe your father has a gun to your head,* I said to myself. *Don't even flinch.* As these words ran through my head, I thought of the military things that I'd learned to do in situations of self-defense, but I simply kept driving and said to my father, "You know where I've been and what I came from before coming here. If you want to live, take that gun from my head." I reached over and took the gun from him while still driving, and again I never said anything to anyone about what happened that day.

This incident happened when Mark was in his thirties, and it drove him further away from his father. This was also the time when he decided to move from the city where he'd been raised and had lived all his life.

Another incident that affected Mark in a bad way happened one day when he heard his mother tell his father not to hit her anymore. He then saw his father raise his hand to hit her, and she shot him in the leg with a gun.

> After seeing my father hit my mother and seeing her shoot him, I made the decision not to ever hit my wife and that I would teach my own boys not to hit girls. People may think kids forget things that happen, but this event stayed with me. Later, after I got married, I even went down some of the same paths of drinking that my father did. After my wife and I divorced, I felt my losses starting to mount up. My life was following the same pattern as my father's.

The biggest turning point of Mark's life came when he was forty. That was when he gave his life to Christ.

> After I gave my life to Christ, I still struggled with the damage that was done to me by my father. One day I felt God say how I can love him and not love my father. My response to God was "I cannot love him, so I guess I cannot love you." About a month after

that I was listening to a preacher on television who said, "You do need to forgive your parents the past and what they did to you. If you want to release and free yourself, you have to release them to God. Tell God how you feel and release them to him." Hearing this took me out of the role of punisher and judge.

I came into agreement with God and told God that if he gave me an opportunity to speak to my father again, I would apologize to him. At that moment, in that same hour, my father called. When I asked my father what he wanted, he said, "I just wanted to see how you are." I told him that I wanted to apologize to him. He asked me, "What for?" "I am just sorry," I said, and his response was, "Don't worry about it." I felt free for the first time.

Mark remarried, and as his father got older and developed signs of Alzheimer's disease, he moved his father so that he could live with him, his wife, and his kids for about a year.

One day while my father was living with me, I asked him why he had asked me to walk with him that day and then left me outside the door for hours.

I went through the whole scenario. My father said, "I don't remember any of that." I thanked God that he helped me forgive and let it go, because I could have gone the rest of my life hating my father for something he did not even remember. I could have ended up killing myself and hurting others. After nearly forty years of hurt and pain, I went from hating my father to committing myself to his care. I hope my story will help other parents realize the lifetime of hurt and pain that can come from a child's home and do whatever they can to prevent it, because not all children survive to tell the story.

My answer to the question "What did your parent do to you?" is that my father gave me a hurt that took a lifetime to heal from. I thank God that I survived it.

A quote from Jawanza Kunjufu's book *Raising Black Boys* is a reminder of how important a boy's relationship with the male in his life is: "Every boy needs a male role model. You can't be what you have not seen. Boys will be what they see."

# CAN THE CYCLE OF DAMAGE BE BROKEN?

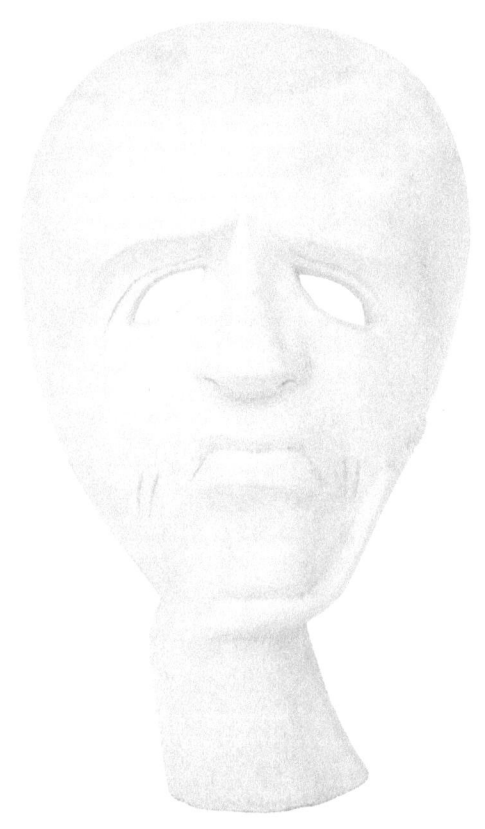

Can we stop the cycle of damaging children? The cycle has to be broken. When a child is abused, he or she may grow up to abuse and hate. These people may hate what they are doing but cannot change their behavior. They may not realize that they are reacting to what happened to them in the past. Many children survive bad experiences with their parents. Most of the people telling me their story said that they never told anyone what they went through. They said that they did not feel that anyone could understand what they went through. Some internalize the experiences because they love their parents and do not want to dishonor or embarrass them.

It is difficult for children to understand how a parent who is supposed to love them and keep them safe can do the opposite. I have found that when children who have been mistreated begin to act out by, for example, fighting in elementary school, abusing drugs or alcohol in high school, or being sexually abusive as adults, they are misunderstood and are thought to be solely to blame for their actions.

## Ruth, age forty-one, raised by a single divorced mother

Ruth, the middle child of eight siblings, was raised by a single mother. She began her story by saying that she just wanted to be healed.

> I am forty-one years old. Why does it still hurt? After you have grown up, a lot of people say you will get over it. When does the healing process begin? I have been through therapy, and no matter how many people I am around, I still feel alone. I have pain every day.
>
> My mother had eight children. I was the fourth child. There are three boys and five girls. No dad, just

my mother with all eight kids, but she was not there for us. Her life was partying and gambling. I know my father, but he never lived with us. We mostly raised ourselves. My oldest sister combed our hair and made sure we went to school.

My mother had different men in and out of her life. A lot of times when she went to sleep, they came in the room and molested us. They would feel me and my sisters and pull our panties down. As we got older, we started to tell my mother some of the things that the men did to us. She brushed it off because they were giving her money. When she gambled, she would stay gone three days to a week. When it got close to the end of the month and we did not have food, we would go to Auntie's house or my younger brother's daddy's house. We went from house to house. We were unstable, so it made my life unbalanced. Even as an adult I feel unbalanced.

Ruth shared that they were always on the run from what she called her mother's men and that she and her sisters had to hide in a closet at night to get any sleep. As a result of what happened to them, they all had problems adjusting to life and to men.

When I got married, I had a problem being approached sexually by my husband, and I tried to commit suicide a couple of times after I had kids. My sisters both do drugs. One of my sisters has ten kids, and another one not only sells drugs but also did drugs with my mother.

My mother moved from house to house, and when I was ten years old, she was into drugs like cocaine. As I got older, I saw her do drugs. I also saw her smoke with a metal thing that I found out later was for drugs. When I was about twelve, the men were still abusing all of us. The men would be in the house and send the boys to the store and then abuse us. This happened for many years. I felt like I was abandoned and that there was no one I could tell. Who would believe me? I felt like my self-esteem and pride were taken from me. Even now that I am an adult, I feel the hurt, and my mother is still not there for me.

When I was thirteen years old, I attempted suicide. I felt that if I took myself out, no one would have to ever worry about me. I cut myself all over my body. I cut my wrist and took every pill I could find. When I was fifteen, I was completely on my own. I stayed with friends, and I did not finish high school.

Ruth had her first child at eighteen. She has three children and said that she tries to give them all of the love she expected out of life. Although it was hard trying to raise the children alone, she thanks God for the role models who have come into her life.

> The thing that gave me comfort was when I was around spiritual people. They reminded me that I may not be all that I should be, but I am not what I could have been. I feel that it is not okay for children to be damaged, even though they can grow up and have therapy. Also, lots of times people look at damaged adults and only see the result of the effect the damage had on them. They do not know the suffering the person has been through that may have caused them to be who they are and to do the destructive things they do to themselves and others, such as drugs and suicide. Society seems to feel that you are doing this to yourself. They do not take into consideration that you may be in a bad place and that you are just trying to survive.

If my mother died tonight, I would say I never had a chance. I would not know what to feel. I have mixed feelings. I don't know what kind of love to have for her because the connection is not there. I respect her and love her like I love others I meet. I treat her the way the Bible tells me to. I thank God for putting people in my life to make up for what I did not get from my parents, but it still hurts. I will not do anything to hurt my brother, but I will patch up the wound that someone else has done.

There are a lot of hurting people out there. Hurt people hurt others. I say to other parents, make sure you love your children and give them spiritual guidance. Cursing and beating causes more damage. When they go out in the street, the street will beat them. Children need to know that no matter what, you love them.

When you ask me, "What did your parents do to you?" my answer is they damaged me for life. They left me damaged goods, but one thing about it—I know there are a lot of people out there just like me who will never get past it. When I look back over my life, I just want to be healed.

Ruth's childhood experiences with her mother have continued to be issues in her adult life. T. D. Jake, in his book *Woman, Thou Art Loosed!*, has a message to inspire women to look deeply for the thing that is draining the life out of them. He relays that Jesus wants to heal the life-draining issues.

> Identify today what it is consuming and draining your life. Then take your "issue" to God. When you move into the fullness of your appointment with God's destiny for you, you won't think anymore about those things that are in your past. You won't have time. You will be so busy raising up your miracle and living in your blessing that all the former things in your life will not only be out of your sight and out of your mind, but out of your heart.

## Maria, age forty-nine, raised by both biological parents

Another life story that was told to me was Maria's story. Maria is a forty-nine-year-old woman with one son in his early twenties. She said that she broke the cycle of damage that was done to her by her parents by not doing to her son what they did to her. When I asked her what her parents did to her, her expression turned sad. She looked me in the eyes and said they abused her.

My mom and dad raised me. There was a lot of physical, emotional, and sexual abuse in our family growing up. The emotional abuse was more from my mother. The sexual abuse was from my father, and the physical was from both.

There were five of us children, and none of us knew that the others were being abused except for the physical abuse. My mom was a very small lady who would say very hurtful, mean things to us. We knew that she knew about the sexual abuse we went through with my father but did nothing about it. At that time there were three girls and two boys. Our brothers suffered the physical abuse, but none of them experienced the sexual abuse that we know of.

I remember the sexual abuse started when I was in kindergarten. I was home from school watching cartoons. My dad came and laid down on the floor next to me. He started watching the cartoons and then just started touching and fondling me. This happened off and on. I found out later in life that my father was doing this to my sisters as well. He was doing this when there were others in the room, but we never knew that this was happening to the other. It wasn't like he would wait until he had us home alone with him. This would happen when everyone was at home.

Maria stated that none of her siblings was ever aware of what was happening to one another. She said her father was very quiet and secretive about the abuse. None of them ever said anything because none of them knew it was happening to anybody else.

As far as I know to this day, with my older sister and me the sexual abuse was just touching and fondling. My younger sister was actually raped by my father, with penetration and everything. This happened to her when she was about thirteen. During the time, my parents were divorced and my father lived in another city. She went to see him for a visitation, and that is when he raped her.

When this happened, he was remarried and with three stepchildren, and they were all in the house. While she was sleeping on the couch, he went out to the living room while his wife was in the bedroom and raped her. I know that there was a situation involving one of his stepdaughters as well. There was an investigation, and he and his then wife were ordered to go to counseling.

The emotional abuse from my mom started when I was very young. One day she made it very clear that she did not like me. When I was in second or third grade, my sisters and I were in the kitchen cooking, and my mother looked at me and said, "I don't like you." I thought she was joking, and she said, "No, I mean it. I don't like you."

Maria said that she and her mother never had a good relationship. Her parents divorced when she was a junior in high school. At that time she told her mother about the father's abuse.

When I told my mother that I felt abused, she said, "Suck it up; it happens to everybody," and she blamed me for the divorce. When she was told about the sexual abuse of my father, she would say things like, "You probably deserved it," or, "If you weren't so bad, it would not have happened." Things got so bad that we all had to go to counseling. During counseling sessions, we found out that my mother had some mental problems because of things that happened to her in her childhood.

Maria stated that the physical abuse was from both parents, who took things to a higher level than just spankings.

An example of the physical abuse is when we were in grade school, my brother and I were about five minutes late getting home on our bikes one evening. We got locked in a box. My father locked us in a big wooden box out in the garage, and we were not allowed to go to sleep. My brother could stay awake, but I couldn't. My dad would come out every hour and hit the side of the box to make sure we were awake. So my brother would let me sleep in his lap, and when he would hear my dad come out, he would wake me up so that I would not get caught.

The physical abuse Maria experienced as a child affected how she parented her son.

With my son I did not want to discipline him. I found myself being overly lenient. When he was about three, he started hitting me, and my friend had to step in and said that what he was doing was not right and that I had to stop him because as he got older, he would still hit me. So I had to step back and say that I can still discipline him without crossing the line like my parents did. My son is now twenty, and we have a wonderful relationship. Everything I went through helped me be a better parent because I knew what I didn't want to do to my child.

When her mother had a stroke, Maria said that the truth was finally revealed. The truth about what her father was doing to her and her sisters came out in the open because the sisters were all together, except for one sister who refused to be around her father under any circumstances.

My older brother did not believe the sexual abuse happened. It wasn't until my dad wanted to visit my sister, who had moved to Texas, and she wouldn't see him, that my brother had to open his eyes. My brother got upset and did not understand why she did not want to see her father. She told him about the sexual abuse, but he did not believe her. Since he and I were close, he called me, and I told him yes, it happened to each one of the girls, and he asked me why I didn't tell him. I said, "What could you have done? You would not have been able to help. You just would have gotten bitten more." So it took awhile for him to come to terms with it because he didn't know.

Now my brother has a family and is doing fine, and my oldest sister is doing fine. But my sister who was raped has had the worst struggle. She has been in a reform school for girls, in jail, and got mixed up with drugs and alcohol. She has also been in one abusive relationship after the other. When I was eighteen, I moved out and had to make myself finish high school. But I left that abusive relationship at home for an abusive marriage. It took me about twelve years to get out of it.

I am now forty-nine, and the one thing I still struggle with today is low self-esteem. It is just from hearing negative things for so long growing up. It still hurts. I keep saying that I deserve better than this and this is what I am going to do. I am going to be better for my son. Both my parents are now deceased.

What did they do to me? They left me an emotionally damaged adult who is determined to break this unnecessary cycle of abuse.

Joyce Meyer is a well-known preacher and author. I have heard her share her story of abuse many times to help others overcome as she has. In her book *Battlefield of the Mind: Winning the Battle in Your Mind*, she inspires her readers not to let anything negative control their minds. She writes that she did not make any progress until she started to believe that she could be set free.

I had to have a positive vision for my life; I had to believe that my future was not determined by my past or even my present. You may have a miserable past; you may even be in current circumstances that are negative and depressing. You may be facing situations that are so bad, it seems you have no real reason to hope. But I say to you boldly, your future is not determined by your past or your present.

# LOVE IS THE KEY

Parents must not be afraid to give and show love to their children. Children need the kind of love that is unconditional. As I stated in the introduction, the definition for unconditional love is affection with no limits or conditions; complete love. The Bible says that God loves us unconditionally. What a wonderful gift! Many adults have never known what it means to be loved unconditionally by their parents. It is difficult to share an experience you've never had. Love is the key to rearing a child to be healthy physically and mentally.

When I look back at the sitcom *The Cosby Show*, I remember there were many people who said the show did not ring true because there were no black families that had parents like that—a father who was a successful doctor and loved his wife and children, and a mother who was a lawyer and who loved her husband.

The Cosbys were portrayed as parents who loved and respected each other and loved their children unconditionally. The parents valued education, and the Cosby children followed their parents' example and went on to college. The show portrayed that children will value what their parents value. Even though the parents had to deal with some of the trials that real families have raising children, they did it with unconditional love. An only child I met was proud to share a little about her upbringing, telling me her story of unconditional love.

## Elaine, age forty-six, raised by both biological parents

My mom and dad raised me. I was in a very stable household. My parents were married for forty-nine years, and they were always together. They are both successful educators who earned doctorates in the field of education. I also had a great extended-family relationship with my aunts, uncles, and grandparents. I would have to say that they all had a hand in raising me, because they all took responsibility for me. I had a large extended family, which consisted of about fifteen aunts and uncles.

To answer the question "What did your parents do to you?" I would have to say that they made me a positive and ambitious person. They accomplished this by introducing me to many positive influences, such as piano lessons and taking me to church. They made me accountable and a well-rounded person by discipline and showing me the importance of education, which was of utmost importance to them.

Elaine's parents taught her how to get along with others by making sure she treated the members of her extended family with respect.

I was an only child, but I had twenty-five cousins on my dad's side and eight cousins on my mom's side. We lived in the same community, so I did not feel as though I was the only child. I had to learn how to share and get along with others at an early age. At school my family was always around, because my dad and mom were in education. My dad worked in the middle school next door to my school. At one point both my mom and dad worked at my school, and in high school my mom was at the same school. I could not get away from them.

Elaine felt that her parents did everything they could for her. She stated that if she could change one thing, it would be for them to have given her more career choices.

I would have liked for them to give me more choices for my life. Back in the seventies, they felt you had to be a doctor or lawyer to be successful. I wanted to be in education like them, but my parents felt that the field of education was not going to take me where they wanted for me. Both of them were from the South. The southern people that I knew had the view that if you had a prestigious position, that meant that you were successful. If they had felt comfortable letting me have a choice, I would have gone a different way with my career. But through it all I knew that they were concerned because they loved me.

I feel that all parents should love their child unconditionally. All my life I felt unconditional love. My dad always told me that "no matter what happens, you can always come home." They had standards, and when I did something wrong, they would be upset. Even when they had to discipline me, I did not feel abused. I know that I completed my doctorate because of the value my parents put on education. They led by example. As a young child I was taken to the bookstore by my dad. He bought me books, which inspired me to read. They taught me to respect myself and others. I know that no one is perfect, but I feel that I had the perfect parents.

What did my parent do to me? They gave me values. Most of all they gave me unconditional love.

After reading the book *Unconditional Parenting: Moving from Rewards and Punishments to Love and Reason* by Alfie Kohn, I felt there was a connection between his meaning of unconditional parenting and the definition I gave for unconditional love. When implementing these concepts, parents have to be genuine and uncompromising. I have found that some parents are afraid that if they show too much love, they may not be taken seriously by their children. In his book Alfie Kohn writes that

Many parents fear that reaching out to develop genuine, warm relationships with their kids may compromise their capacity to control them. Much of conditional parenting can be traced back to the fact that when those two objectives clash, control tends to be favored over connection.

## Elizabeth, age fifty-nine, raised by biological mother and father

Is it possible to grow up in a house with several siblings and the same parents and yet have different experiences than your siblings? Elizabeth shared that her answer to what her parents had done to her would be different from the response her siblings would give. She said that she has always wanted to talk about her experience growing up but did not think anyone would believe her.

> I do not know how it happened, but I did not get as damaged as some of my sisters and brothers. As an adult I have listened to them talk about some of the negative experiences that they had in our home. I was unaware of a lot of what they said happened. I did witness the arguing and cussing fights that my

parents would have all night and on the weekends. When my father came home drunk, I would be frightened and could not sleep. I also remember praying that they would not kill each other.

Elizabeth said that when she thought about her childhood, she mostly remembered feeling loved. When she became a teenager, things changed in such a negative way, she was left very confused. The following is what she expressed of her journey of confusion, accomplishment, and forgiveness.

My parents are from the South, and they had a lot of children for two reasons. First, they had us on purpose, and secondly, they did not have birth control available to them. They started having children in the late forties and finished in the early sixties. All seven of us are one to two years apart. I believe that as my mother had baby after baby, her love for us filled the house.

I believe that my mother had a lot of children because to her, children meant that you would have someone to take care of you when you were old. She also believed that it was possible for us to do something worthwhile to make money and even become famous by being the first to accomplish something great.

When I was a young child, up to the age of about thirteen, my mother and father would ask us what we wanted to be when we grew up. I would say a doctor, and they would get me a doctor's kit for Christmas. My mother always told us we could be the first to accomplish things in life, like the first woman astronaut. I grew up knowing that I wanted to do something to make my parents proud of me. I also wanted to grow up and be able to take care of them and buy them a house, etc.

When we were little, my mother and father would pile us all into the car (station wagon) and take us for rides through the upper-class neighborhoods, and as we looked at the beautiful homes, they would tell us that we could live there someday. Even though we were poor, we did things as a family and I did not feel poor. On the weekends they would take us on rides to the airport to watch the planes come in and to the drive-in theater. In the summer we would pack up the station wagon and go out of town to visit my mother's relatives.

Both of my parents had a good sense of humor. They loved to laugh. My father had cute nicknames he would call my mother, and she would smile. My mother had games she would play with us when we were little kids that would make us laugh and run around the house. My father worked two to three jobs and my mother was a stay-at-home mom until we were in our teens. I remember being hungry and waiting at the door for my father to come home with food. My mother served my father his food first, and we would say grace at the table before we ate.

My father's mother was responsible for having us in church. She was one of the mothers of the church, and it was her mission to make sure that we all knew about God and got baptized. When my mother was troubled, I would see her lower her head, but I never saw her cry. I feel that I got my strength from her and my grandmother. My mother taught us a prayer to say each night before we went to bed—"Now I lay me down to sleep, I pray the Lord my soul to keep, if I die before I wake, I pray the Lord my soul to take."

The older we got, the more things changed. I saw my father become a bitter man. He had a house full of teenage girls, and he did not know what to do with us. His way of handling us was with accusations. He accused us of doing drugs and having sex. I was not interested in doing either at the time. As a teenager I was confused and afraid of him most of the time. And then it happened. We started having babies, and some of my siblings even started doing drugs. I had a baby girl my senior year in high school. My father was determined that it was time for us to get out of the house and started this campaign before any of us was ready or prepared.

My siblings have told stories of seeing violent acts from my mother and father and of being abused physically and mentally by my father—experiences that I did not witness, but I believe them because I have seen the result of the damage done to them by their experience with my parents, such as drug and alcohol abuse.

My sisters and brothers also have a different attitude about life than I do. I am an optimist, and most of them are pessimistic and judgmental. My younger brother is the only one that I can truly trust and communicate with. We both have a relationship with God and a forgiving spirit.

By the age of twenty I was a single mom with two children. After having my second child, I was living on my own and experiencing financial and emotional hardship. My second child's father was living with his mother, working and making a good income. His mother asked me if they could take my son. I said no, and for months I tried to keep us all together. Finally I thought it would be best for my son if he stayed with his father and grandmother until I got on my feet. I told them that the arrangement was temporary. For the next months I took my daughter to visit with him, and I looked forward to having him back home.

Unfortunately, this was not to be. I received a call that my son had been injured in an accident and died by the time they got him to the hospital. I felt pain that I cannot describe. I covered my head and walked around in the state of grief for a long time. People around me became concerned and started to make attempts to help me. I received the help I needed from two things—the grace of God and my love for my daughter. When I looked at her, I knew I had to survive.

The worst experience that I had with my father was after I had moved out and had had my second child. I started coming over and spending a lot of times at my parents'. Because of this, my father thought I wanted to move back and threatened to slap me during a conversation we were trying to have about it. At that point I left my parents' house. I did not come back for a long period of time.

My life was not an easy journey. When I look back, I know that I was not equipped. I went through drinking alcohol to deal with stressful times in my life. I did not get involved with drugs, but thank God I survived many other bad decisions. I was very protective of my daughter and wanted the best for her. I decided to be an example to her and my nieces and nephews by continuing my education. I felt that just because I did not have an example did not mean that I could not be an example.

I finished high school, and later as an adult I went to college. I earned a total of four degrees, which consisted of a bachelor's degree in teaching, a master's in school administration (school principal), and a PhD in education. My mother died at the young age of sixty and did not see me earn any of my degrees. She was in my thoughts with each accomplishment, especially my doctorate. I know she is proud of me.

My father came to my graduation celebrations when I received my bachelor's degree and master's degree. He also came to each of the family Christmas celebrations at my home before he died. He lived to be in his eighties. Before he died, I asked him about the time he threatened me, and he said that he did not remember the incident but that he was sorry. I told him that I forgave him. I actually had forgiven him years earlier when my mother was dying in the hospital. He came to the hospital every day for two weeks and was not drunk or drinking. He was there for us, and I never forgot it.

My answer to the question "What did your parents do to you?" is they loved me the best way they knew how.

In *Unconditional Parenting*, Alfie Kohn also wrote,

Children will still look up to us even if we're candid about our limitations, even if we speak to them from our hearts, and even if they can see that, for all the privileges and wisdom that adulthood confers, we're still just people struggling to make our way in the world, to do the right thing, to balance people's needs, to keep learning—just as they are. In fact, the more real we are with them, the more likely it is that they'll feel real respect for us.

# INTERVENING FOR A BROKEN CHILD

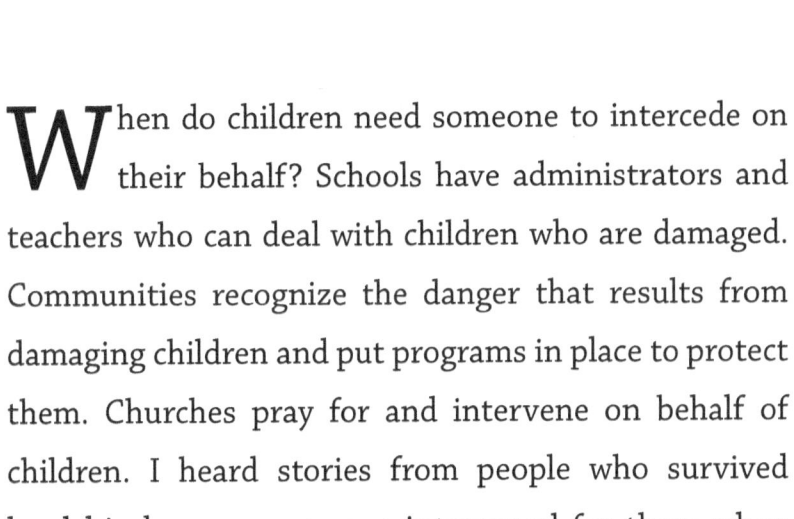

When do children need someone to intercede on their behalf? Schools have administrators and teachers who can deal with children who are damaged. Communities recognize the danger that results from damaging children and put programs in place to protect them. Churches pray for and intervene on behalf of children. I heard stories from people who survived hardship because someone intervened for them when they were children. As an example of what it means to intervene on behalf of a child, I have taken those stories and created one about a young man who was homeless.

## Lamont, age thirty, raised by his mother's sister and her husband

After being kicked out of his mother and father's home at age fourteen, Lamont had nowhere to go and was embarrassed to tell anyone.

> As a child I was physically and emotionally abused by my father. I was also sexually abused by my uncle—my father's brother. My father's father physically abused him as a child as well. I remember my father coming home late at night and pulling me out of bed and beating me and calling me names for no reason. When my mother tried to stop my father from hitting me, he would turn on her and start hitting her. One night I was sitting on the family sofa watching television, and Father came in the door, walked over to where I was sitting and hit me in the face, and said, "What are you looking at?" This hit was the breaking point. I decided that he would never hit me again. I fought back and ran out of the house. At this point I knew I could never go back home.

For a couple of months Lamont stayed overnight at friends' houses but did not stay long enough for them to start asking questions. He spent time with a female friend who liked him. He was staying in her bedroom without her parents knowing he was there. After six months his friend became very ill, and he took her to the emergency room.

The doctor informed my friend and me that her sickness was due to the fact that she was pregnant. I was very upset because we had engaged in sex, but we did not have serious feelings for each other. As a matter of fact, I was very confused about my sexuality, and I believed it may have been because of the sexual abuse in my life. Now I felt like an abused and confused teenager who was going to be a parent.

When my friend and I received the news from the hospital, my friend—who was also fourteen years old—began to cry. We talked and cried together for days. Finally I decided that we had to tell someone, so I went to my aunt, my mother's sister. My aunt and her husband were active members of a local church. My aunt looked at us two young people and said that we were still just children and decided that she would intercede on our behalf. She spoke to her husband and with the permission of my mother went through the necessary steps to become my legal guardian. I am not sure how she got my mother's permission, but I am sure that conversation was ugly.

Lamont's aunt took him at a hurtful time and brought him to live with her.

My friend who was pregnant told her family about the pregnancy, and they decided not to allow her to have the baby. Her parents took her out of the city they lived in to get an abortion. I was hurt and very confused about their decision, because I was not given the right to an opinion in the matter.

While living with my aunt, she took me to church on Sundays and to different events that the church would have. My aunt's husband became a mentor to me. As a result I grew up to develop a relationship with God. After completing high school, I went on to college. I am thankful to my aunt and her husband, who interceded on my behalf when I was a fourteen-year-old child. Because of their intervention, I developed a relationship with God that healed me of the damaging effects of the abuse I experienced with my father and his brother, my uncle.

When asked "What did your parent do to you?" my response would be that my father put me in the position to meet a man of God who saved my life and that God's grace gave me strength to forgive my father and uncle.

The article I referenced in the introduction from the *Columbia Electronic Encyclopedia*, titled "Child Abuse—Causes and Effects 2012," sheds light on some characteristics of abusers.

In some cases abusers do not have the education and skills needed to raise a child, thus increasing the likelihood of abuse and providing inadequate parental role models for future generations. Abused children are more likely to experience generalized anxiety, depression, truancy, shame and guilt, or suicidal and homicidal thoughts or to engage in criminal activity, promiscuity and substance abuse. There are many interacting causes of child abuse and neglect. Characteristics of circumstances of the abuser, the child, and the family may all contribute. In many cases the abuser was abused as a child.

# A HEALING EXERCISE

If you were asked what your parents did to you and you could answer freely, what would your answer be? Take a moment and think about it. Think about the experiences you had with your parents when you were growing up. Your experiences might have been negative, positive, or both. Ask a friend the same question, and you will find that you both have a lot to share.

Before you tell your story to someone else, you may want to write it. Writing your story is a way to organize your thoughts as you recall things that happened. Most importantly, recalling and reflecting on your childhood story can be freeing. What might have made you feel like you were keeping a secret no longer has a hold on your mind. Find a private place and a quiet time to ponder and reflect. As you make the journey back through your childhood, ask yourself questions such as "Why did I go there at that time?" or "How old was I when that happened?" The questions will cause you to reflect back. By doing so, you can find answers that will enable you to continue to build the events of your story.

Be honest with yourself. Don't add anything that did not happen. If you can't remember something, make a note of the lost memory as part of your story. It is okay not to recall every detail of what occurred. It does not make your story any less true or important if you can't. Whatever you discover about your childhood, remember that the experiences you had with your parents played a large part in shaping who you are, the way you act as a parent, and why you respond to life the way you do.

- You may decide not to share your story with anyone.
- Reliving the experiences that you had with your parents can be healing.
- You may find reasons to appreciate and celebrate your upbringing.
- You may find doors that need to be closed.
- You may find that you need to forgive so that you can move on.

## A Healing Exercise

Get rid of all bitterness, rage, anger, harsh words, and slander, as well as all types of evil behavior. Instead, be kind to each other, tenderhearted, forgiving one another, just as God through Christ has forgiven you (Ephesians 4:31–32 NLT).

# Final Reflections

While many things can happen to us that play a role in how we enter our adult lives, none are as powerful as the experiences we have growing up with our parents. As I stated in the introduction, my definition of a parent is anyone legally responsible for the health and well-being of a child. The adult with whom the child lives and is under the care of is responsible for the types of experiences the child will have.

Most of the people answered "What did your parents do to you?" by sharing negative experiences. I believe that their stories make real the damage that can be done to children by parents. There are also stories that express the positive effects of unconditional love that parents can give their children.

Their childhood experiences, whether positive or negative, played a part in the types of adults and parents they have become. As previously mentioned in the introduction, other outside influences affect the outcomes of our lives, but the focus of this book is on the experiences children have with their parents.

As I reflect on the stories I've heard, I find that some adults survive the negative experiences they had as children. Their survival may not be easy, and it may take them through a lifelong journey of healing and forgiveness. Many are determined to stop the cycle of damage in their families. They do this by not repeating their parents' actions. Their determination causes me to ponder the possibility for every child to have the best chance possible to grow up well-rounded, whole, and undamaged.

Is it possible not to have to spend your adult years healing from wounds obtained during a dysfunctional childhood? There are children who may never know what it means to have unconditional love, but this type of love does exist in homes. Love is the key to parents producing children who grow up to be socially and emotionally healthy.

I pray that as you read these stories, you appreciate why they were told. In many cases, these people had never told their stories to anyone. They also deeply felt that their journeys through life were strongly affected by the positive and negative experiences they had with their parents. My final reflections on their stories also helped me realize the distress some of them went through just by telling their stories. Sharing their stories was not easy, because they had to allow themselves to relive some very painful experiences.

Still, they all agreed to tell their stories with the hope that they would make a difference. Allowing others to see through the windows and behind the closed doors of their childhoods might cause other parents to stop and think about how they are interacting with their children. For some, telling their stories was healing, while for others it was a way to appreciate and celebrate their lives.

# Bibliography

Angelou, Maya. *Mom & Me & Mom*. New York: Random House, 2013.

*Columbia Electronic Encyclopedia*, 6th ed. Accessed June 3, 2013. www.infoplease.com/encyclopedia/society/child-abuse-incidence.com.

Dictionary.com, s.v. "unconditional love." Accessed June 3, 2013. http://dictionary.reference.com/browse/unconditional love.

Jakes, T. D. *Woman Thou Art Loosed!* Ada, MI: Bethany House Publishers, 1996.

Kohn, Alfie. *Unconditional Parenting: Moving from Rewards and Punishment to Love and Reason*. New York: Atria Books, 2005.

Kunjufu, Jawanza. *Raising Black Boys*. Sauk Village, IL: African American Images, 2007.

Meyer, Joyce. *Battlefield of the Mind: Winning the Battle in Your Mind*. New York: Hachette Book Group, 2003.

## About the Author

Mattie Lee Jones, PhD, for over 20 years, Dr. Jones has been involved in the education of countless Indianapolis children, including work as a teacher and a school administrator (e.g. principal). Her work as a University Professor has afforded her the opportunity to develop programs involving child development, early childhood education and teacher preparation. Her abundance of experience with children and parents motivated her to pen her first book "Missing Link?" that documents various parents' perspectives concerning the education of their children? Her experience training and supporting child care workers and providers motivated her to pen "Disciplining Someone Else's Children (A guide for Child Care Providers)" which is a fact-based guide to discipline for preschool children. Her book "NURTURE" derives from the desired to continue to support the social, emotional and cognitive development of children by connecting the social and emotional development of children to learning. Dr. Jones's book "What Did Your Parent Do to You" reveals true stories that open windows to how childhood experiences influence the journeys people take thru life as well as how they parent. Dr. Jones earned a K-12 Teacher degree from the University of Indianapolis; a Master's degree in K-12 Educational Administration from Ball State University, Muncie, Indiana; and a PhD in the Philosophy of Education from Indiana State University, Terra Haute, Indiana. She is an active member of organizations that support the social. emotional and cognitive development of children and serves as a child outcomes consultant.

www.ingramcontent.com/pod-product-compliance
Lightning Source LLC
Chambersburg PA
CBHW020128130526
44591CB00032B/566